Francis Frith's
Around Belfast

Photographic Memories

Francis Frith's
Around Belfast

Henry Hall

FRITH
BOOK Co

First published in the United Kingdom in 2000 by
Frith Book Company Ltd

British Library Cataloguing in Publication Data

Around Belfast
Henry Hall
ISBN 1-85937-094-2

Frith Book Company Ltd
Frith's Barn, Teffont,
Salisbury, Wiltshire SP3 5QP
Tel: +44 (0) 1722 716 376
Email: info@frithbook.co.uk
www.frithbook.co.uk

Printed and bound in Great Britain

Front cover: Castle Place 1897 40187

Acknowledgements

All the information in the notes which accompany the photographs is readily available, if one
knows where to find it: I am grateful for the help given to me by the staffs of the Linen Hall
Library, The Central Library, Belfast, (in all its sections), The Ballynahinch Library Headquarters
and the libraries at Bangor, Carrickfergus, Gilnahirk and Larne.
Essential help came from the Lisburn Museum and the Heritage Centres at Bangor and Larne.

Several of the following books consulted were found for me by the librarians and curators:-

Harry Allen & Bill Pollock - Donaghadee
Jonathon Bardon - History of Belfast
John Barry - Hillsborough
May Blair - Once Upon The Lagan
Keith Haines - Campbell College
Paul Larmour - Arch Guide to Belfast
Brian Mackey - The Market House and Assembly Room, Lisburn
Grenfell Morton - Railways in Ulster
Grenfell Morton - (Ed) - Victorian Bangor
W M Sayers - Reminiscences of Old Bangor
Edmund Whitehouse - British Dance Bands

Contents

Francis Frith: *Victorian Pioneer*

FRANCIS FRITH, Victorian founder of the world-famous photographic archive, was a complex and multitudinous man. A devout Quaker and a highly successful Victorian businessman, he was both philosophic by nature and pioneering in outlook.

By 1855 Francis Frith had already established a wholesale grocery business in Liverpool, and sold it for the astonishing sum of £200,000, which is the equivalent today of over £15,000,000. Now a multi-millionaire, he was able to indulge his passion for travel. As a child he had pored over travel books written by early explorers, and his fancy and imagination had been stirred by family holidays to the sublime mountain regions of Wales and Scotland. 'What a land of spirit-stirring and enriching scenes and places!' he had written. He was to return to these scenes of grandeur in later years to 'recapture the thousands of vivid and tender memories', but with a different purpose. Now in his thirties, and captivated by the new science of photography, Frith set out on a series of pioneering journeys to the Nile regions that occupied him from 1856 until 1860.

Intrigue and Adventure

He took with him on his travels a specially-designed wicker carriage that acted as both dark-room and sleeping chamber. These far-flung journeys were packed with intrigue and adventure. In his life story, written when he was sixty-three, Frith tells of being held captive by bandits, and of fighting 'an awful midnight battle to the very point of surrender with a deadly pack of hungry, wild dogs'. Sporting flowing Arab costume, Frith arrived at Akaba by camel seventy years before Lawrence, where he encountered 'desert princes and rival sheikhs, blazing with jewel-hilted swords'.

During these extraordinary adventures he was assiduously exploring the desert regions bordering the Nile and patiently recording the antiquities and peoples with his camera. He was the first photographer to venture beyond the sixth cataract. Africa was still the mysterious 'Dark Continent', and Stanley and Livingstone's historic meeting was a decade into the future. The conditions for picture taking confound belief. He laboured for hours in his wicker dark-room in the sweltering heat of the desert, while the volatile chemicals fizzed dangerously in their trays. Often he was forced to work in remote tombs and caves where conditions were cooler. Back in London he exhibited his photographs and was 'rapturously cheered' by members of the Royal Society. His reputation as a photographer was made overnight. An eminent modern historian has likened their impact on the population of the time to that on our own generation of the first photographs taken on the surface of the moon.

Venture of a Life-Time

Characteristically, Frith quickly spotted the opportunity to create a new business as a specialist publisher of photographs. He lived in an era of immense and sometimes violent change. For the poor in the early part of Victoria's reign work was a drudge and the hours long, and people had precious little free time to enjoy themselves. Most had no transport other than a cart or gig at their disposal, and had not travelled far beyond the

boundaries of their own town or village. However, by the 1870s, the railways had threaded their way across the country, and Bank Holidays and half-day Saturdays had been made obligatory by Act of Parliament. All of a sudden the ordinary working man and his family were able to enjoy days out and see a little more of the world.

With characteristic business acumen, Francis Frith foresaw that these new tourists would enjoy having souvenirs to commemorate their days out. In 1860 he married Mary Ann Rosling and set out with the intention of photographing every city, town and village in Britain. For the next thirty years he travelled the country by train and by pony and trap, producing fine photographs of seaside resorts and beauty spots that were keenly bought by millions of Victorians. These prints were painstakingly pasted into family albums and pored over during the dark nights of winter, rekindling precious memories of summer excursions.

The Rise of Frith & Co

Frith's studio was soon supplying retail shops all over the country. To meet the demand he gathered about him a small team of photographers, and published the work of independent artist-photographers of the calibre of Roger Fenton and Francis Bedford. In order to gain some understanding of the scale of Frith's business one only has to look at the catalogue issued by Frith & Co in 1886: it runs to some 670 pages, listing not only many thousands of views of the British Isles but also many photographs of most European countries, and China, Japan, the USA and

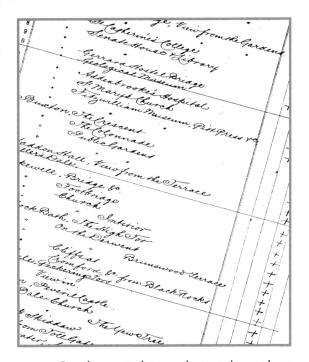

Canada – note the sample page shown above from the hand-written *Frith & Co* ledgers detailing pictures taken. By 1890 Frith had created the greatest specialist photographic publishing company in the world, with over 2,000 outlets – more than the combined number that Boots and W H Smith have today! The picture on the right shows the *Frith & Co* display board at Ingleton in the Yorkshire Dales. Beautifully constructed with mahogany frame and gilt inserts, it could display up to a dozen local scenes.

Postcard Bonanza

The ever-popular holiday postcard we know today took many years to develop. In 1870 the Post Office issued the first plain cards, with a pre-printed stamp on one face. In 1894 they allowed other publishers' cards to be sent through the mail with an attached adhesive halfpenny stamp. Demand grew rapidly, and in 1895 a new size of postcard was permitted called the court card, but there was little room for illustration. In 1899, a year after Frith's death, a new card measuring 5.5 x 3.5 inches became the standard format, but it was not until 1902 that the divided back came into being, with address and message on one face and a full-size illustration on the other. *Frith & Co* were in the vanguard of postcard development, and Frith's sons Eustace and Cyril continued their father's monumental task, expanding the number of views offered to the public and recording more and more places in Britain, as the coasts and countryside were opened up to mass travel.

Francis Frith died in 1898 at his villa in Cannes, his great project still growing. The archive he created continued in business for another seventy years. By 1970 it contained over a third of a million pictures of 7,000 cities, towns and villages. The massive photographic record Frith has left to us stands as a living monument to a special and very remarkable man.

Frith's Archive: *A Unique Legacy*

FRANCIS FRITH'S legacy to us today is of immense significance and value, for the magnificent archive of evocative photographs he created provides a unique record of change in 7,000 cities, towns and villages throughout Britain over a century and more. Frith and his fellow studio photographers revisited locations many times down the years to update their views, compiling for us an enthralling and colourful pageant of British life and character.

We tend to think of Frith's sepia views of Britain as nostalgic, for most of us use them to conjure up memories of places in our own lives with which we have family associations. It often makes us forget that to Francis Frith they were records of daily life as it was actually being lived in the cities, towns and villages of his day. The Victorian age was one of great and often bewildering change for ordinary people, and though the pictures evoke an impression of slower times, life was as busy and hectic as it is today.

We are fortunate that Frith was a photographer of the people, dedicated to recording the minutiae of everyday life. For it is this sheer wealth of visual data, the painstaking chronicle of changes in dress, transport, street layouts, buildings, housing, engineering and landscape that captivates us so much today. His remarkable images offer us a powerful link with the past and with the lives of our ancestors.

Today's Technology

Computers have now made it possible for Frith's many thousands of images to be accessed almost instantly. In the Frith archive today, each photograph is carefully 'digitised' then stored on a CD Rom. Frith archivists can locate a single photograph amongst thousands within seconds. Views can be catalogued and sorted under a variety of categories of place and content to the immediate benefit of researchers.

Inexpensive reference prints can be created for them at the touch of a mouse button, and a wide range of books and other printed materials assembled and published for a wider, more general readership - in the next twelve months over a hundred Frith local history titles will be published! The day-to-day workings of the archive are very different from how they were in Francis Frith's time: imagine the herculean task of sorting through eleven tons of glass negatives as Frith had to do to locate a particular

See Frith at www. frithbook.co.uk

sequence of pictures! Yet the archive still prides itself on maintaining the same high standards of excellence laid down by Francis Frith, including the painstaking cataloguing and indexing of every view.

It is curious to reflect on how the internet now allows researchers in America and elsewhere greater instant access to the archive than Frith himself ever enjoyed. Many thousands of individual views can be called up on screen within seconds on one of the Frith internet sites, enabling people living continents away to revisit the streets of their ancestral home town, or view places in Britain where they have enjoyed holidays. Many overseas researchers welcome the chance to view special theme selections, such as transport, sports, costume and ancient monuments.

We are certain that Francis Frith would have heartily approved of these modern developments in imaging techniques, for he himself was always working at the very limits of Victorian photographic technology.

The Value of the Archive Today

Because of the benefits brought by the computer, Frith's images are increasingly studied by social historians, by researchers into genealogy and ancestory, by architects, town planners, and by teachers and schoolchildren involved in local history projects.

In addition, the archive offers every one of us an opportunity to examine the places where we and our families have lived and worked down the years. Highly successful in Frith's own era, the archive is now, a century and more on, entering a new phase of popularity.

The Past in Tune with the Future

Historians consider the Francis Frith Collection to be of prime national importance. It is the only archive of its kind remaining in private ownership and has been valued at a million pounds. However, this figure is now rapidly increasing as digital technology enables more and more people around the world to enjoy its benefits.

Francis Frith's archive is now housed in an historic timber barn in the beautiful village of Teffont in Wiltshire. Its founder would not recognize the archive office as it is today. In place of the many thousands of dusty boxes containing glass plate negatives and an all-pervading odour of photographic chemicals, there are now ranks of computer screens. He would be amazed to watch his images travelling round the world at unimaginable speeds through network and internet lines.

The archive's future is both bright and exciting. Francis Frith, with his unshakeable belief in making photographs available to the greatest number of people, would undoubtedly approve of what is being done today with his lifetime's work. His photographs, depicting our shared past, are now bringing pleasure and enlightenment to millions around the world a century and more after his death.

Around Belfast – *An Introduction*

Belfast is no ancient town. For centuries this part of Ireland was dominated by the castle at Carrickfergus; there was also a small castle at what is now Belfast to watch a ford across the river. It was when the Scottish and English colonists began to populate the counties of Antrim and Down that the spot at the head of the Lough became an obvious place to develop a town. Sir Arthur Chichester was given the castle and the surrounding lands in 1603, and work seems to have started soon after. The settlement was not much older than that to be founded by the Dutch at New York.

The rapid growth of marketing and trading soon brought an inn, and in 1682 a bridge of 22 arches was being built to cross the river. Everything was under the control of Chichester. When he became Lord Deputy of Ireland, Belfast was made one of the 40 new Irish boroughs, which were each able to send two members of parliament to Dublin. Both of Belfast's members were the choice of the Chichester family for several generations. Before the end of the century, the head of the family was given the title of Lord Donegall, and there are still street names everywhere to recall the event.

A town such as this had to be self-sufficient, and a whole range of manufacturers came into being. As a port, considerable agricultural exports were handled, and long-standing links were made with Scotland and England. Belfast the industrial town was brought into being by textiles and shipbuilding. In the 1770s cotton, then a protected Irish industry, yielded to manufacture by machinery; it was here that there was the business acumen and capital to build the first Irish mill. More followed, and as a result local engineering benefited. The vessels built by the Lagan were getting bigger, and in 1821 one was launched embodying the latest idea: it was a sail-boat aided by a steam engine, which foretold of an enormous contribution to the Belfast scene. Then linen manufacture became a mechanised process, and Belfast made the most of a world-wide market. When the 1897 photographs were taken, the mills employed something like 50,000 workers.

The photographs, therefore, tell of a city very much alive and prosperous. It had recently grown at a rate far exceeding that of any other such place in the British Isles; its 300,000 inhabitants meant it had added something like 75% to its population in 25 years. On top of the tens of thousands at work in the linen industry, the money-spinners were the shipyards, where the largest employed nearly 9,000 men who delivered 11 sizeable ships during the year. Outside the yards were several engineering works supplying the world. If Belfast had the largest flax-spinning mill in the world, it also boasted the largest purpose-built tobacco factory.

These essentials of wealth were backed by an extensive harbour that was still adding new docks. There were also three main-line railway terminals; the housing needs for all the people were being met, along with their new churches; and for the better off there were handsome villas, and the department stores in the town.

The Frith team were to return to Belfast in later years; included in this selection are photographs from 1936, which add to the story.

Castle Place 1897 40187

High Street 1897 40175
This was the first street in the town to be built, but it had long lost its residents when this view was taken. It was now a shopping street, with the buildings of fairly recent date providing commercial office accommodation on the upper floors. The shops were for the better-off, as the lady in her trap and the man-servant holding the horse show. The establishments were mostly family-owned, with the proprietors living among their customers in the new outer suburbs. The three delivery vans outside Forster Greens shows the service to be had; this was only one of their two premises in town. In the High Street there were as many as 15 shops selling clothing and footwear. However, the very success of it all was inviting change: only five doors beyond Forster Greens was a shop owned by Thomas Lipton. A Glasgow man born of Clonnes parents, Lipton's object was to sell large quantities of tea at a low price through branches throughout the British Isles. Already a multi millionaire, he enjoyed membership of the Bangor Yachting Club. Within a year he was to be knighted by the Queen. The forest of poles above No 16 marks the telephone exchange, staffed by operators waiting for incoming calls before pushing in the plug to make the connection. It also tells of the ongoing battle between the private National Telephone Company and authority, both Parliament and local. The Post Office already owned the telegraph system, and wanted its hands on the telephones. Parliament had given powers to the Company to lay wires under the streets, but local authorities, including London, refused to have their streets dug up. (Number 16 is still there.)

High Street 1897 40176

The broad thoroughfare reflects not only the market town but also its link with the sea. Below the cobbles still runs the Belfast River, which once had quays allowing ships to come off the Lagan. The far, tall building marks Bridge Street, the spot where the first bridge upstream was located. The shape of things to come is the brand-new National Bank building; this bank had a London base boasting capital of £7m, and several branches in Ireland. Two doors before the bank is the ancient Skipper Street, occupied by houses and the homes of a group of boot and shoe manufacturers. The last premises on the right are those of the chronometer makers F M Moore. The clock mechanism of the Albert Clock had been made here. The accuracy of the time shown on the ten-foot dials was kept under observation by the firm with the aid of an electric signal box from Greenwich, using the under-sea Telegraphic Cabling System. The success of these cables owed much to the scientific genius of William Thompson, born in College Square, Belfast and now Lord Kelvin. Any establishment with a cross-channel trade now had its telegraphic address to which messages could be tapped.

Castle Place 1897 40187

The horse-drawn trams were a long-established feature of the city, and the system was still being extended up the Cregagh and Anderstown Roads. All parts could be reached from this corner, and its popular name of Castle Junction had become fixed. The 114 cars and 1,000 horses were the property of the Belfast Street Tramway Company. The company was now ready to bring in electric trams, and had an act of parliament approving the work. However, this was subject to having the approval of the Corporation, which was not forthcoming. As things stood, the company operated under a lease from the Corporation under which it paid rent for the use of the streets. The Corporation had just gained some experience in supplying electricity for light in the city centre from a station in Chapel Lane. The demand of the trams would make it all the more worth-while to carry on with plans to build a more substantial power station on East Bridge Street by the river, using imported coal. Without doubt, the councillors' thinking was influenced by their experience of running a gas works at a very good profit. Even then, it was producing the money to build a splendid new City Hall, which was to become the perfect memorial for those years. The company made three offers to the Corporation, including one with profit sharing, but to no avail. With another seven years for the lease to run, the city had to wait until 1905 for the new trams.

Queen's Square 1897
40178

Its quays were once the heart of Belfast the port, and there is no doubt that the remains of Chichester Quay on the right and Hanover Quay on the left will be found below the cobblestones. The square had reached what was to be the height of its dignity, though the row of buildings on the left was modest enough. Some of its very old houses survived until recently. Air raids in 1941 destroyed the fine Georgian buildings opposite the Customs House. Commerce and travellers were served by the stand of jaunting cars. Another car stand at Botanic Gardens contributed £10 towards the cost of the Queen Victoria Statue now in front of the City Hall.

◀ **Victoria Street 1897** 40180
This view shows Victoria Street at the crossing with Ann Street, heading for Queen's Bridge. The telephone wires must also have been going over the river. The groups of people in conversation do not suggest any danger from traffic, but the helmeted policeman, on view to all, was ready to deal with any snarl-ups that might occur during the day.

◀ **Victoria Street 1897** 40179

▼ **The Albert Clock 1897** 40182

Queen Victoria was 42 when her consort died. She grieved her loss for the rest of her long life, and the Kingdom mourned with her. She symbolised a nation that was the great maritime empire-builder and the workshop of the world. For Belfast, the monument had to be fitting and the subscription generous. Work began in 1865, and it took four years to complete. The statue of the Prince is 40 ft above the ground, and the near two-tonne bell could be heard eight miles away on quiet days. The clockwork is to the same design as that of Big Ben. The clock's central position at the foot of High Street meant diverting the underground River Farset. The foundations did not quite meet the problem: although the photograph does not show it, a tilt had already developed.

◀ **Victoria Street 1897** 40181

Here we see another view of the street, which was cut in early Victorian times to become a channel of trade and industry. The vista extends to Cromac. The nearest building, owned by the Scottish Amicable Assurance Society, was the first such independent block designed to make its impact on Belfast. If the Lloyds office adds to the prestige of the establishment, then it seems no harm was done by accommodating a band-room. The lower building marks the corner with Queens Square, and belonged to the Northern Bank. If it was to be left behind in height, its stone still befits the solidity of a bank.

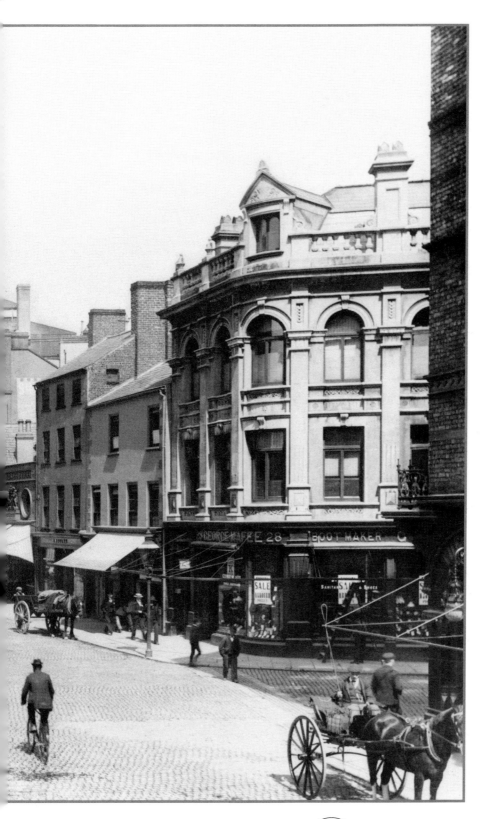

Corn Market 1897

40184

This street-name reminds us of Belfast the market town: the view looks from Arthur Square (another Chichester name). Since the famine and the ending of the restrictive corn laws, grain was largely an import handled by a number of merchants. The curved building on the left is brand-new. The building at the end of the view is a prosperous department store in High Street. The row on the right tells of a not-so-distant past: these are clearly old houses left behind, now forming shops and protected by the essential awning.

Royal Avenue 1897 40186

During the 19th century, the well-laid-out streets to the south beyond Donegall Square were matched (at least in orderliness) by those built on the reclaimed land near York Street. In between, there remained a triangle of small slum streets beginning at Castle Place. In 1878 the Town Council obtained powers to clear the area; they began by extending the town centre with a fine new street connecting Castle Place with York Street. There was already the beginnings of a route in one very old narrow street, but all signs of Hercules Street were to disappear, along with its 40 fleshers and their killing yards. Four thousand people were to lose their homes, but it was said that they would have no difficulty in finding somewhere else to go. The same confidence ordained that the thoroughfare was to be 80ft wide and lined with tall buildings built to a uniform height. These were to be fronted with shops to create a first-rate retailing zone. The councillors were right to name it Royal Avenue. The photograph shows the Provincial Bank, which had in fact been in 'Hercules Place', now absorbed. Its railings and shrubs helped to put it in line with the new Avenue, and it became number 2. It was listed among the five best bank buildings in Belfast. Next is the Ulster Reform Club, marking the real start of the Avenue. Those who formed it looked to the great Mr Gladstone to bring changes in society; but even as the Club was being built, it became known that he had now decided to give Ireland a devolved government, with a Parliament in Dublin. The club became the gathering point of the Liberal Unionist Party. The next domed building was very new in 1897; the dome marked the luxurious 200-bedroom Grand Central Hotel. This was the essential hostelry of all important visitors to Belfast for many generations.

Royal Avenue 1897 40185

This shows the far end of the Avenue, looking into York Street. Forster Green clearly thought the length of the street was the right distance from his Castle Place headquarters to site another branch. The clothing shops had awnings to fend off fading from the powerful sun. The upper floors of the blocks were given over to offices catering for the total life of the busy town. The windows of the Unionist Association can be seen; there were also at least six trade union tenants along the way, and two of the big English railway companies had ticket offices. Neither of those ran ferries to the port. The largest category of tenants was those dealing with the ramifications of the clothing trade. Another indication of improved standards of living was the large number of solicitors and insurance agents. Everything seems to have operated on a small scale, and no doubt with much footwork as well as letter-writing. Telegrams could be sent from the massive General Post Office Building. A few offices would have telephones - but all would need their fireplaces, as the rows of chimney-pots show.

Donegall Square North 1897 40189

The elegant emporium of Robinson and Cleaver (centre) tells of a Belfast upper crust, which had to be catered for. It was one of many commercial buildings taking over the residential square. The diminutive building just beyond it, at the other corner of Donegall Place, was now the Royal Hotel, but it had been built by Lord Donegall as his town house. The massive linen warehouse nearer the camera was one of the first big buildings to take over the square; it marks what linen meant to Belfast. It was built soon after the American Civil War - at that time the industry prospered, since Lancashire was starved of cotton. It was owned by Richardson Sons and Owens, whose extensive mills and factories were at Bessbrook in County Armagh. These Quakers had built a model village there, which was to be taken as a pattern by others in England.

The Harbour Office 1897 40220 ▶

Belfast had a very effective body managing and improving its harbour long before it had a council able to provide roads, drainage and oversee housing. This was the office of the Harbour Commissioners, a body of senior ship owners, shippers and merchants; they did away with the small docks to provide spaces now occupied by Queens, Albert and Corporation Squares. They established the basis of the present harbour. A major task was the cutting of the Victoria Channel to give a straight passage from Queens Bridge to the Lough. The work left an island where they built a slip, which was soon to be managed by J E Harland. In 1897 the commissioners were landlords to a yard employing nearly 9,000 on the County Down side. The astonishing trade of Belfast, and the charges on ships and goods, provided all the money required and some to spare. The non-profit-making commissioners built these handsome offices. Well furnished, with marble busts and the walls hung with pictures, the decor would have become a London gentlemen's club. They designed a uniform for formal occasions: frock coats, white waistcoats and fancy buttons with gilt anchors. Not all was harmony, however; there were battles to be fought with their shipbuilding tenant across the river.

◄ Ann Street 1897 40188

It was a ford which fixed the site of Belfast, but not long after the town was begun, a bridge crossed the river. The approach to it, Ann Street, was the second most important thoroughfare; beyond the bridge it took the name Bridge End. The 120ft glass kiln in the background of this photograph was already over 100 years old, and the tall chimneys show that Ballymacarret had its other industries. The single-track tram rails must have been enough to serve the areas up to Knock and Belmont. A stop just over the bridge would have been convenient for Queens Quay railway station.

▲ Corporation Square 1897 40177

The broad straight streets tell of land recovered from river and docks. The church tells of the human needs that followed. It was as early as 1832 that the Seamen's Friendly Society was set up; by 1836 it had a small building of its own in Pilot Street. In 1848 it became part of the Presbyterian Church in Ireland, and a few years later it was decided that there should be a new congregation. At the same time a wealthy shipper died, and his widow asked for a church to be built in his memory. The Sinclair Seamen's Presbyterian Church we see is the work of the leading Belfast architect John Lanyon. The minister was always to devote part of his time to seamen, and 50 seats were reserved for sailors. The Seamen's Friendly Society was to have a voice in church affairs. A few years after this photograph was taken, the church came under the care of a man who began to furnish the interior with nautical emblems. The bowsprit pulpit is still there, complete with bow and starboard lights. He persuaded the congregation that it would not be sinful to sing hymns at public service.

▼ **The Customs House 1897** 40223

This photograph shows the splendid elevation of a building which never got the formal square it deserved. It had an added fame in those years when the flight of steps provided an open-air dais for speakers on religion, politics and strike action. The cobblestones held listeners in their thousands, while the Royal Irish Constabulary watched for feelings becoming dangerous. The low door on the right marked the chief telegraph office of Belfast, and in 1870 it was open seven days a week from 6am to 3am by Greenwich Mean Time.

▼ **The Custom House 1897** 40221

This is the elevation to Donegall Quay, with the entrance for the masters of ocean-going ships coming to report their arrival with goods which had to pay duty. This early morning view shows the Grand Central Hotel's courtesy coach waiting for visitors.

▲ **Canal Wharf and Queen's Bridge 1897** 40225
The wharf tells of another watery enterprise. The River Lagan flows within a few miles of the huge Lough Neagh, which is bordered by four Ulster counties; a lot of work was done to make the river able to take barges, with a link to the lough. It was never very profitable, but it carried a considerable amount of traffic until well after this photograph was taken. Most of the traffic carried coal, which was loaded in the harbour beyond the bridge and taken to the linen mills along the river, but there was also a steady flow of sand downstream to this wharf. The barges made the first part of their journey upstream with the aid of steam tugs; here we see a tug returning to the coal quays - its funnel would be lowered to miss the arches. The long 21-arch bridge built across the Lagan in the 17th century served for a very long time; it was Victorian Belfast which built this five-arch Queen's Bridge. It had to be widened not very long before the photograph was taken, and the massive brackets that carry the pavements can be seen.

The Custom House 1897 ▶
40222
The two cannons were captured from the Russians in the Crimean War. On the other side of the quay were the mooring points for the ferries plying to Glasgow, Liverpool, Heysham and Fleetwood. The low arched door led to a basement store where imported goods could be held until duty was paid.

◀ **Belfast Royal Academy 1897**
40191
There were already several schools in the town when the Minister of the First Presbyterian Church in Belfast advertised the arrival of a new academy. It could take boarders, and must have been intended for the middle classes. The first School building was constructed not too far from the church in what was to become Academy Street. Discipline was strict, which caused a revolt when some boys took food from the kitchen and barricaded themselves in, armed with pistols. Armed men were brought to force a way in.

The Ulster Bank, Waring Street 1897 40203

This splendid building must have overawed the narrow Waring Street, which could only lay claim to such a pile because of its very long history as a place where business was to be done. Waring Street is very near and parallel to High Street, and is shown on very early maps. For those coming into town by way of Donegall Street or North Street, it gave quick access to the first docks.

Belfast Royal Academy 1897 40192

Situated at the corner with Donegall Street, and very near the parish church, the academy was in a pleasant enough part of the town. It was not to stay that way, and no provision had been made for privacy or expansion. During the course of the 19th century, the street filled with the homes of skilled workers, along with a variety of yards and a wash-house. The numbers of pupils fell dramatically.

Belfast Royal Academy 1936 87676 ▶

All this was put right in 1878, when the move was made to this fine building. This time the position was right: it was about one and a half miles out of town, and set in the new suburbs along the Cliftonville Road.

▼ The Ulster Institute For The Deaf, Dumb and Blind 1897 40202

This handsome edifice catered for those needing help from all over the province. It once stood on University Road opposite Queens University. When it was new in 1845, it was described as being on the new Lisburn Road about a furlong from the turnpike. Its 225ft frontage, along with two wings extending to the rear, shows what could, and had to be done, by charity. At the time there was a substantial income; but the estimated cost was seven times greater, and a further appeal had to be made. The satisfaction of the subscribers was ensured by employing the leading Belfast architect, and clearly he was not restricted in his art. The foundation stone was laid by Lord Donegall, using a silver trowel.

▼ Queens College 1897 40201

When this building was opened in 1849, it faced the almost-new Deaf and Dumb Institute; the two buildings extended this edge of Belfast, bringing a formal touch to it. Not yet an independent university, the college was one of three set up by the government; they were linked to the Royal University of Ireland, which operated as an examining body from Dublin. The other two colleges were at Cork and Galway. The object was to increase the supply of men with higher education; it was hoped to attract entrants from all religions, with no theology being taught. Facilities were to be made available to all churches to instruct their own students. As it was, there was the 250-year-old Trinity College in Dublin under the control of the Established Church, and the Catholics had been provided with Maynooth College in 1795. In the recent past the northern Presbyterians had been refused government help to erect their own co-establishment to prepare men for the ministry, and were building their own nearby. They then provided Queens with its president and deputy president, as well as a number of lecturers. The Catholic Church would not support Queens at all. This photograph shows all that was built at the beginning; there is no evidence yet of local pride in the shape of buildings paid for by industry, including the Harland Engineering Laboratory. Eleven years after this view was taken, the independent Queens University of Belfast was created.

▲ The Methodist College 1897 40198

There was an urgent need for this school for the sons of Methodist ministers, for the ministers were re-located every three years. The project had occupied the church authorities for some years, who had Dublin or Portadown in mind. But when fifteen acres of ground became available at the foot of the Malone Road, the plans were completed.

◄ The Methodist College
1897 40199

A Limerick architect provided the design of the building, though his estimates of cost proved to be low - help from the all-powerful American Methodists was welcome. The college opened in 1868, taking 80 borders and 120 day boys, not all Methodists. It soon became the largest school in Belfast. Some years later, additional accommodation was provided in the McArthur Hall; this was named after its benefactor, who was Lord Mayor of London and a Westminster MP.

◀ **Campbell College 1897** 40194
This splendid establishment was three years old in 1897, and had been created by a fortune left by the bachelor R J Campbell. His trustees bought the Belmont Estate on the eastern edge of the city; there was ample money to provide the very best, with well-furnished science laboratories, a gymnasium and dormitories with individual cubicles.

▼ **Campbell College 1897** 40195

◄ **Campbell College 1897** 40193

◄ **Campbell College 1897** 40196
The college opened with 80 borders and 20 day boys. Almost at once something went wrong - there was no lack of teaching skills, but the managerial expertise needed was not there. The inevitable stress led to seven members of staff being required to resign, and one of them took the matter to court. The press reported the business in full.

Elmwood Church 1897 40204
Nothing demonstrates the wealth of Belfast more than its ability to build fine churches ahead of the press of growing suburbs. Elmwood church was built in 1859, and shared the open ground on that side of town with Queens College and The Institute for the Deaf, Dumb and Blind. At a safer distance across open fields were the grim blocks of the Workhouse. The design of the tower displays the hand of the amateur architect.

Antrim Road 1897 40190

This photograph was taken to capture the early days of the Antrim Road as a superior residential area of Belfast. Castleton Terrace, near the camera, is still there; it is typical of the handsome rows lining the road to enjoy views of the Cave Hill and the Lough. Fortwilliam Church had taken its name from the adjacent park, which had large mansions, complete with gate houses, coaches and coachmen. On the main road, the prestige was largely shared by the new side avenues, complete with their front railings to give a sense of order to the scene. The horse-drawn tram system terminated here, but a walk of a few yards brought one to the steam-engine-driven Cavehill & Whitewell Company's trams.

◄ **Belfast Castle
and Cavehill 1897** 40215

When Lord Ashley married Harriet Chichester, the only surviving child and heiress of the third Marquess of Donegall, his father may have made it plain that if he was to become an Irish landlord he would expect him to be a good one and no absentee. His father was the 7th Earl Shaftesbury, the famed philanthropist, who fought for several acts to protect industrial workers. The most famous was that which stopped very small children working down the coal mines - the statue of Eros in Piccadilly Circus marks a nation's gratitude.

Ashley's father-in-law built this castle shortly before selling Ormeau House to Belfast Council. On his death, the Ashleys started to make visits and became involved in local affairs. Charities were supported, and a garden party was held for local notables. Their son inherited the title of the 9th Earl Shaftesbury and the estate. He married

Lady Constance Grosvenor, a member of the Duke of Westminster's all-powerful family. Despite the grandeur Constance had known as a Grosvenor, she was delighted with Belfast Castle. Perhaps she had never known a parkland which soared up over 1000ft to enclose the massive Cave Hill. From the mansion there are splendid views across the Lough, and in Constance's time, many of the ships going to and from the Belfast Harbour were under sail. All day, too, the trains could be seen puffing their way to Londonderry and Larne - the Victorians loved their railways.

The pair lived a lot of their time here, and became immersed in the life of Belfast. He became an Alderman, and then Lord Mayor. He was Lord Lieutenant of County Antrim, and became the first Vice Chancellor of Queens University. Their regular visits were ended by the First World War. In 1934 the castle and park were given to Belfast.

◄ **Belfast Castle and Lough 1897** 40214

◄ **Belfast Castle and Cavehill 1897** 40216

▼ **Cave Hill and the Castle 1897** 40217

A good snatched view can be obtained of this 1200ft mountain from the pavement outside the Belfast City Hall, which is less than three and a half miles away. To get just the contour he wanted, Frith got himself into the Belfast Waterworks and captured the hilltop, the aristocratic castle and an expanding suburb.

▼ **Ormeau Park 1897** 40206

This park was the first open space secured for public recreation in Belfast. There was an initial problem, in that the law in Ireland dealing with such things did not allow the necessary action, so this had to be attended to. That done, the Council knew what it wanted: it approached Lord Donegall to see if he would let them take over the house and park at Ormeau.

▲ **Ormeau Park 1897**
40207
Lord Donegall was quite willing, since he had just built the new Belfast Castle on the Antrim side of the town. He was not going to live at Ormeau again, and was gratified to know it was to be put to public use. His agent thought the rent of £10 an acre was too low, but the deal went through in 1869 and 178 acres were taken over.

◀ **Ormeau Park 1897** 40208
100 acres was considered
enough for a park, and the rest
was made available for what
was to become Park Road with
North and South Parades. The
park at that time edged the
river, but a road has now been
built. The 'peoples' park' was
opened in 1871 amid scenes of
great jubilation. Later, a local
lady complained that she could
not send her children to the
park with their nanny because
of rough youths, so two park
constables were appointed.

◀ **The Botanic Gardens 1897**
40210
The park had only been in public hands a short time when these photographs were taken. It had been owned and developed by the Royal Belfast Botanical and Horticultural Society for its members to enjoy and stock with the natural spoils of the Empire. It began in 1827, when a 14-acre farm was bought from Lord Donegall. In 1840 a long conservatory was built, and 12 years later the palm house was added.

◄ Alexandra Park 1897 40219

This park was the third in Belfast. It opened in 1885, with ten more acres being added later. There was no park in the north end of the town, but the opportunity was there in the shape of some unwanted land. The banks of a short stretch of Milewater had once provided clay for bricks, tiles and a pottery. There was a pond, which caused legal difficulties: the nearby linen mills had rights to the supply of water, and the delays made some councillors impatient for the work that would be provided for the unemployed. 1885 was the year of the visit of the Prince and Princess of Wales, and the park took the name of the Princess. The row of houses stretching up to the Antrim Road has the name Jubilee Terrace, celebrating the Golden Jubilee of Queen Victoria in 1887.

▲ The Botanic Gardens 1897 40212

Its expenses were met by the subscriptions of the members, fees from letting others use the park, and an exhibition hall. Over the years its affairs do not seem to have been very well managed; by the time a liquidator approached the Council, there were five public parks in the city and the exhibition hall was no longer in demand. The agreed purchase money cleared substantial debts, but there were some complaints that there were enough parks. Oddly enough, the arguments in favour thought it would be greatly appreciated by the gentry of the district.

◄ The Botanic Gardens 1936 87687

The 'Dynamic' 1897 40230
This ship was one of a fleet of six owned by the Belfast Steamship Company. She was one of its express boats, which provided a nightly service to Liverpool from Donegall Quay. Cargo went from York Dock. Behind can be seen the crammed yard of Harland and Wolff, where the 'Dynamic' had been built 14 years earlier. In 1897 eleven new ships were delivered, including the 'Pennsylvania' for the Hamburg Amerika Line - according to the Belfast Newsletter, the largest in the world.

The Douglas Boat 1897 40232
This was the Royal Mail Steamer plying to the Isle of Man; it had just left the quay at Belfast at 4pm. On summer Sundays there was more work to be done by the boat, with 'Holiday Tours' to Liverpool or Dublin calling at Douglas. The Belfast and County Down Railway used their Slieve Bearnagh trips to Portrush or Portaferry with cruises up Strangford Lough.

The Glasgow Boat 1897 40233
The Royal Mail Steamer 'Adder' made the link with Glasgow by sailing to Ardrossan. This avoided the long journey along the Clyde Estuary - the route was completed by rail. For this daylight crossing, the train will have left Glasgow central at 9.07am with passengers arriving at Princes Quay at 4pm. The vessel was not very old; perhaps conditions at Ardrossan dictated the use of paddle propulsion at a time when screw had become the norm.

▼ **Belfast Boat Club, River Lagan 1936** 87671
This club house was opened in 1898 by Mrs W J Pirrie, wife of the managing director of Harland and Wolff; among the well-wishers was Mr Gustav Wolff, also representing Belfast craft of a larger size. The club was 23 years old, and had 300 members to share 'the delightful pastime of rowing'. The lower dock could accommodate the club's 'fleet' of 24 pleasure boats, but racing boats had to tie up at St John's Wharf. A speaker appealed to Belfast Council to complete the scene by building a dock in the Ormeau Park where it bordered the river. The band of the North Staffords provided the music, and the view shows that music was part of the arrangements in 1936.

▼ **View on The Lagan 1936** 87672
Parts of the Lagan Canal were cuts made to pass wide bends in the river, but most of the route is the river itself, with the tow-path added. It makes its way along the lovely Lagan valley; some of the most beautiful stretches are within a short distance of Molly Ward's Lock. All hustle was left behind, and the walker could enjoy the snipe and kingfisher. This is all now part of the Lagan Meadows nature trail.

▲ **The Lagan Canal, Stranmillis 1936** 87674
For those who could not join the Belfast Boat Club, with its tennis court and long tea-room, there was still the canal to be discovered at Stranmillis. Here was the beginning of the canal: the boats are moored just above No 1 lock, the first of 27 needed to reach Lough Neagh. The smoking chimneys tell of the cramped homes of the river people - in their parlance they were at 'Molly Ward's Lock'. Up to this point the barges had navigated the wide, tidal river above the Belfast coal quays pulled by steam-engined tugs.

◀ **View on The Lagan 1936**
87675
This view of the Lagan Canal has all the appearance of a Sunday afternoon, with no risk of getting in the way of the horses and their tow ropes. It could also have been so quiet because Belfast residents had so much choice when the time came for the essential walk.

The Zoo and Amusement Gardens, Bellevue 1936 87679
When Belfast took over the tramway system to Glengormley, it found itself possessed of property outside the City boundary, along with some very attractive terrain sloping up to the mountains. The forceful manager of the tramways persuaded his committee to find the money to create paths to form a leisure park. Some years later, a report told of a very profitable tram route, with people 'flocking' to enjoy the park. When the adjoining Hazelwood Estate became available, this same committee took it over and worked hard to bring about what we see here. The house itself was now a café/restaurant.

The Floral Hall, Hazelwood 1936 87677
This building at Hazelwood was brand-new when the photograph was taken. It looks as if it was intended for Portrush, and is an enthusiastic example of the architecture of the time. It also reflects the social history of Belfast: to begin with, it was referred to as a concert hall, but to the young people of the next 25 years, it was a ballroom, and its isolation never detracted from its fame. They went to waltz, quick-step and fox-trot to orchestras which included violins as well as saxophones and trombones.

Lisburn

Lisburn, Market Square 1896 L138001

When Frith went to Belfast it was not his intention to record its industries, but he knew he had to take note of the fame of the fabric known world-wide as Irish Linen. He was sent to Lisburn, where the industry had all begun. Lisburn was already established when the French refugee Louis Crommelin arrived with the latest expertise in making linen. A long period of prosperity is shown in this view of the Market Square - the Tuesday market had been going on for 268 years. The church had cathedral status, and its structure is an example of Plantation Gothic. Its slim steeple tells of a Georgian's ideas on the style. The tower, with its clock and cupola, mark a market house and assembly rooms, which have a history of their own. It was only seven years since the town's landlord had embellished the edifice to what we see. Another reminder of Sir Richard Wallace is the cast-iron ornamental fountain. It was one of fifty or so which he commissioned; most of them were erected in Paris, where he lived, to celebrate the end of the siege of the city by the Prussians in 1871.

Hillsborough

**Hillsborough,
The Court House 1890** H14202

Here we see another view of the splendid Court House. Begun in 1772 as a market house, it seems to be a centrepiece for the vast County Down estate. The big house (the castle) was not yet begun, and it came without a long drive. The two are within sight of each other and complete the picture. There are fine houses looking on to take their share. The view down the hill can bring in the hills beyond Belfast Lough; it could once have played a part in communications to bring aid as required.

◄ **Hillsborough,
Main Street c1890** H142006
The statue is of the fourth Marquis of
Downshire, the 11th descendant of the
Hills of Hillsborough. He inherited estates
amounting to 75,000 acres in County
Down, 16,000 in County Wicklow, 4,000
in Kings County, 9,500 in County Antrim,
2,100 acres in Kilkenny and 1,355 acres
in Kildare. There were also 5,600 acres in
England. His term also coincided with the
great famine. He did not leave Ireland. 'I
will stand by the people and attend to
their wants even should I be obliged to
mortgage my last acre'. The main street is
lined with comfortable houses as befits a
well-managed estate, which brought in
improved agricultural methods and
established the linen industry.

◀ **Hillsborough, The Court House c1890** H142005

The Court House overlooks a square which was once alive with traffic. As well as the Mail Coach, there were several private coach companies running between Dublin and Belfast. The Royal Corporation Hotel not only provided refreshments and accommodation, but it also produced the essential change of horses for the fast-running services. Before the railways, journey time was getting close to twelve hours, and the road surface shows what was needed.

▼ **Hillsborough, Main Street 1890** H14201

This photograph shows a town that has had its changes. The lamp tells of a long-established gas works; the railway came not long afterwards. The mile-post on the hill still tells of 70 miles to Dublin, but those are Irish miles. The estate was in the hands of Lord Arthur Hill and his nephew, the sixth Marquis, who was to come of age in 1892. This young man was to see the end of the old Irish landlord/tenant relations. Sale to the farmer was not yet compulsory, but a 100% loan could be obtained, with the repayments less than the old rent. The Seventh Marquis sold the house to the new Government of Northern Ireland to become the residence of the Governor of the province in 1924.

◀ **Hillsborough, Hillsborough Castle c1890** H14203

This 18th-century house links the family with the first Hill arrivals. It stands on the foundations of a fort built about 1639 by Sir Arthur Hill after he left a post at Carrickfergus Castle. It was given Royal approval and the garrison was paid for. King William stayed there on his way to the Boyne. About 70 years later this house was begun; despite its delicate, fashionable doorway, it was a Crown establishment. It still allowed its store of arms to be taken by the dissidents of 1798. In 1890 the Government was complaining of the continuing cost, and his Lordship compensated with a lump sum. The garrison were allowed to end their service.

◄ **Carrickfergus,
The Town c1897** 40280
The Normans established a town, and
provided the church which was
dedicated to St Nicholas. Carrickfergus
was to share the tumults which the
castle brought, but the town we see
here was busy and prosperous, with
markets twice a week and five linen
mills needing workers. The harbour
would have exported the rock salt,
taken from four deep mines, to be
processed across the water by their
owners. The linen would have gone by
rail to the specialised warehouses in
Belfast. The main line belonged to the
Belfast and Northern Counties Railway,
but there was a locally-owned
Carrickfergus Harbour Junction Railway.

Carrickfergus

Carrickfergus, The Castle 1897 40276
It was a hundred years after the Normans defeated the English at Hastings that they had ambitions to conquer Ireland. The system required castles to proclaim dominion, and the huge slab of rock jutting into the lough and named Krag Fergus gave an ideal site. The work John de Courcy began in 1180 was meant to signify that everything had changed, but unlike most castles, it was not to bring peace. These stones were to witness turmoil and violence over many centuries. This photograph was taken from the old pier where King William landed in Ireland on his way to do battle at the Boyne.

Carrickfergus, Fisherman Quay c1897 40281
The quay was built in 1830 for the men who lived in the overlooking Scotch Corner. When this picture was taken the fishing industry was no longer important, but according to a local historian of the time it had once provided work for something like 300 people, counting those employed on secondary parts like net-making. The photograph shows the strange massive blocks of limestone used in the pier's construction. Some of the details are still to be seen, including the steps from which the boat is pulling away.

Carrickfergus, Looking North East 1897 40282
Most of these houses are still there, but no longer depending on the Battery Wall for protection from the sea. This is the Joymount corner of the town; the gardens, no longer there, mark where a governor of the castle, Sir Arthur Chichester, began to build a fine mansion in 1610. Sir Arthur died in London in 1624, but was buried in the church of St Nicholas, where there is a wonderful Jacobean monument to him and his wife. In 1898 the town's landlord was Lord Shaftesbury; the estate came to him from his father marrying the surviving Chichester daughter. When he married, the tenants of Carrickfergus sent a deputation to congratulate him.

Whitehead

Whitehead, The Beach 1897 40295
This sea front was hard to negotiate, despite all the signs of a developing resort. The railway, which had been pushed into a tunnel to get round White Head, had also trapped the village against the sea. However, a new station was now planned with a sizeable refreshment room; behind that was growing a town decidedly Edwardian in style. It was becoming a favourite place for the seniors in Belfast City Hall and the port - to say nothing of a host of sea captains.

Whitehead, ▶ General View 1897

40290

This shows the town, the railway and the headland. The first station had been provided only 20 years before. It soon became a destination for those who wanted to enjoy a spot which seems to make the mouth of Belfast Lough its own. County Down embraces the scene from the Copeland Islands until the Hollywood Hills merge with White Head. The far view is completed with the full run of the Rhinns of Galloway. This was the very place to see the many big sailing vessels which still went to and fro.

**Blackhead,
The Town 1897** 40296
At 15 miles from Belfast,
this was the obvious
destination for the day
tripper. This perfect
walking territory is within
yards of the town. The
railway company was still
working to extend the
path round Blackhead,
and the shelters have
the unmistakable stamp
of railway architecture
about them. Soon it was
claimed that the visitors
amounted to thousands.
There was no sign yet of
the lighthouse, which
was to be erected by the
Commissioners of
Irish Lights under
pressure from the
Belfast Shippers.

Larne

**Larne, McNeill's Hotel ,
Main Street c1890** L142001
The train from Belfast would get you to Larne and
on your way to London with a total journey time of
13 hours. The same line brought you to the starting
point of the wonderful Antrim Coast Road. The
excitement and style portrayed in this scene make
modern experience dull. It seems the terms for this
comfortable-looking hotel had held for some years.

▼ **Larne, The Town Hall 1900** L142011
This substantial civic building was the gift of a local J P, and befits a leading Irish
port serving the daily Royal Mail run to Stranraer. There was also a ferry running to
Glasgow bi-weekly, to Ayr tri-weekly and to Liverpool weekly. The town was the
first in Ulster to use electric street lighting; this lamp illuminates what was then the
T-junction of Main Street and Cross Street. The public house is still in place.

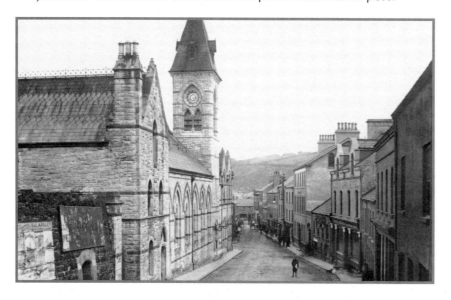

▼ **Larne, The Promenade 1900** L142010
Here is Larne the holiday resort, with its own segment of the rugged Antrim Coast.
The promenade sports two bathing piers, one for ladies and one for the gentlemen,
each complete with changing accommodation. The replica ancient Irish round
tower is a memorial to a local M P who died in the prime of life. 92ft high, it carries
navigation lights. On the other side of the entrance to the lough and harbour is the
Ferries Point Lighthouse standing on an unspoilt Magee Island.

▲ **Larne, Boyd's Shop,
Main Street 1900** L142012
Mr Boyd had clearly set his
stall up to catch the eye of
the visitor with spades for
the beach along with gifts
and photographs to take
home. His advertising
seems aimed at his Larne
customers; the door on the
right took you not only to
dressmaking, but also a
wide range of drapery and
Irish linen. He had his own
new photographic studio,
and those world departures
catered for the immigrant.

◀ **Larne, Glynn Village c1890** L142002
Francis Frith would have been directed to the village of Glynn as the 'artists' spot'. Only three miles from Larne, and hard by the Lough, there was the complete rustic setting of winding streams and picturesque ruins. He saw what he wanted in this winding street of thatched cottages, and just needed the helpfulness of the driver to bring the thing off.

Larne, Main Street 1900 L142015
Whether arriving from the harbour or the Glenarm Road, this was the first view of the aptly named Main Street. Nearly a third of a mile long, it now shows off the town's electricity with poles to carry the lighting and telephone system. Although incidental to this scene, the substantial Laharna Hotel was the first feature to catch the eye. The top storey was a recent addition in response to the growing popularity of the short sea route.

Bangor

Bangor, The Front 1897 40250
Brighton made the seaside fashionable for the
upper crust, and its wider popularity was settled
when the railway made the connection in 1841. The
Belfast & County Down Railway was running to
Newtownards by 1850, but did not see any reason
to bring Bangor into the system until 1865. For
those who made the short sail out from Belfast, the
charms of this piece of coast were obvious: a bay
lined with low, craggy rocks and sands providing
picturesque bathing pools. As always, the railway
made all the difference; the mansions on the skyline
were followed by accommodation for those who
could afford to get away from it all for a spell.

Bangor,
The Esplanade 1897

40253

This shows the heart of the Victorian holiday town, with the required esplanade and gardens for strolling. But there are links with an older Bangor: the wide space once held cotton mills when that was a protected industry in Ireland. There was a pier, and no doubt American cotton could be brought from Belfast, and coal for the boilers would come direct from Scotland and England. The pier had been provided by the landlords. Their mark on the scene is the stone-built Tower House to the left of the terraces. It was built in 1637, soon after the charter from James the First brought the Scots to make the new plantations.

▼ **Bangor, General View 1897** 40238

This is the view the big houses saw, with the new rows of houses which had helped to add nearly 50% to the town's population in ten years. The handsome ornament at the corner of the wall of Kensington Villa is still there, somewhat damaged, but not yet ten years old at this time. The steeple belongs to the first Presbyterian Church, and to the left can be seen the growing mass of the Parish Church of St Gomgalls almost ready to take its steeple. The dedication of the church recalls an ancient Bangor. Not long after St Patrick brought Christianity to Ireland, a monastery was founded here by St Gomgall. It was he who sent out missionaries to those corners of Europe lost to paganism.

▼ **Bangor, The Steamer 'Sleive Bearnagh' 1897** 40237

For most of the century there had been daily steamers from Belfast to Bangor, and as the holiday traffic increased the County Down Railway took over the service. Their ships came onto the route in 1894, leaving Belfast at the 'Bangor Jetty' near Queens Bridge. The next year the railway built the long new pier seen here. During the 12th July holiday week, the ship called at Bangor and then went on to Larne. Return tickets to Bangor could be used by the holder to return to Belfast by rail. To increase the attraction of a pier to the casual pedestrian, a band stand stood at the seaward end.

▲ **Bangor, Main Street 1897** 40267

Here we see another view of the main street. The jaunting car tells of the recent changes, and the lamps tell of a gasworks only waiting to be expanded. Along with the ice cream shop, there were other shops springing up to cater for holiday-makers. If greater prosperity meant that more people could take a week's break, there were still many more who were left behind. They could share something of what went on by the arrival of a picture postcard. Better still, a search among the novelty shops would find just the right gift to take back.

Bangor,
Main Street 1897 40266
The workaday appearance of the street shows how it had been overtaken by the success of the resort. These houses would have been built when Bangor the port had to deal with a constant stream of sailing ships bringing in coal and limestone and carrying away lead and copper ore, along with locally-made bricks and tiles. One of the three piers in 1897 had a crane to lift out the coal. All such places had their 'Commercial Hotels' to suit the Victorian commercial traveller arriving by train to show his suitcase of samples.

Bangor, The Esplanade 1897 40241 This shows the New Pier, and the foot of the 'old pier' complete with its own attraction in the form of a coffee stall. The day seems to have been warm enough to keep the ice cream vendor busy. Perhaps it was warm enough to persuade folk to take a jaunting car rather than face the uphill walk to the station.

◀ **Bangor,
Bowman's Terrace 1897** 40259
Acclaim meant numbers, and
somehow the town was taking in
enough visitors each summer to
double the winter population. The
challenge was met by new
boarding houses, tall and each
able to take in several families.
They were built in rows.
Bowman's Terrace was one of the
earliest, claiming space hard by
the sea and near the town. It
made the corner for Somerset
Avenue, a name which with
others like Tennyson Avenue,
Southwell Road and Holborn
Street, might have brought a
touch of the supreme Brighton.

◄ Bangor, The Bathing Place 1897

40264

Sea bathing and swimming were now fashionable; here Bangor could hardly be beaten, with its rocky pools and coves. The local landlord had spent money to improve on the situation, as can be seen from the platform and diving board. This was a lovely spot for the ladies to observe the sport, and even for two to join in. For the less daring an umbrella keeps off the damaging effects of the sun.

▼ Bangor, The Grand Hotel from the Old Pier 1897   40261

Here we have a range of hotels for those who could afford the comfort. The Grand was almost brand-new, and the Royal was rebuilding. Another recent pile was Pim's Stores, ready to cater for the same clients. The Stag's Head ranked as a public house, but took visitors. It stands at the corner of Ballymagee Street, a name which was not thought quite suitable; it eventually became High Street. The handsome Ulster Bank adds dignity to the row, even though it belonged to the more practical Bangor - it overlooks the coal pier with its office. Another touch of industry is lent by the massive iron vessel with its lifting gear.

◄ Bangor, The Terraces 1897   40258

The block at the corner is one of the latest boarding houses, and has clearly pushed back some older buildings. No doubt the kiosk sold tickets for the boats at the end of the pier, but for a generation which knew nothing of cars it also led to a railway system opening up the delights of County Down. It was a very attractive feature for the growing number of cross-water visitors.

Donaghadee

Farewell To Donaghadee

Will anyone here undertake to deny,
That a difficult matter is saying goodbye?
I would rather if possible limit my song,
To the hope of returning before very long.
Although I am going to bid you goodbye,
I beg you will not take the trouble to cry;
A farewell, for the present I mean it to be,
Farewell, for the present, to Donaghadee.

Farewell to the harbour, farewell to the moat,
And the boating - farewell to it - not that I boat;
Farewell to the seat where I often have sat,
Farewell to this room for the matter of that.
Farewell to the Copelands, I never was there,
Farewell to the perfume of flax in the air;
Farewell to the musical sounds of the sea,
Farewell to the people of Donaghadee.

When St Patrick set sail for this isle of the West,
He considered the shortest sea passage the best;
And St Patrick and I are inclined to agree,
For, the shorter the passage, the better for me.
So if to revisit you I should contrive,
In one thousand eight hundred and seventy-five,
I venture to hope that my journey by sea,
Will be straight from Portpatrick to Donaghadee.

Anon. Published 1874

◄ **Donaghadee, The Beach 1897** 40285
The bay marks the natural harbour of this spot. It is
also the point where the town looks across to
Portpatrick; the two islands are not 22 miles apart,
and a long history of travel between the two was
unavoidable . A busy port became the Royal Mail
route, and then came the beautifully-engineered
harbour and a lighthouse. That was nearly 80 years
before this photograph was taken, and it was the
days of sail. Almost at once, the steam ships began
to take over; other places were more suited to that
kind of shipping. Local enterprise brought the
railway up from Newtownards and Belfast, but
Donaghadee had become a place to enjoy, rather
than a working port.

Donaghadee, The Wharf 1897 40286
This photograph shows the town clinging to the sea with some lines of very small cottages. The mound is man-made, and was very likely first topped by a Norman fort. It was still there for the Scots planters to add their plan and get the approval of James I (the sixth of Scotland) for the new port.

Donaghadee, The Imperial Hotel 1897 40287
The Imperial must have been the largest of the several hotels catering for the traveller as well as for the more frequent tripper from Belfast. The number of tall boarding houses was still growing. The Parish Church has Norman foundations. The new clock had been given by the De Lacherois family, and tells of the presence of the local squirearchy.

Index

Frith Book Co Titles

Frith Book Company publish over a 100 new titles each year. For latest catalogue please contact Frith Book Co.

Town Books 96pp, 100 photos. County and Themed Books 128pp, 150 photos (unless specified) All titles hardback laminated case and jacket except those indicated pb (paperback)

Around Barnstaple	1-85937-084-5	£12.99
Around Blackpool	1-85937-049-7	£12.99
Around Bognor Regis	1-85937-055-1	£12.99
Around Bristol	1-85937-050-0	£12.99
Around Cambridge	1-85937-092-6	£12.99
Cheshire	1-85937-045-4	£14.99
Around Chester	1-85937-090-X	£12.99
Around Chesterfield	1-85937-071-3	£12.99
Around Chichester	1-85937-089-6	£12.99
Cornwall	1-85937-054-3	£14.99
Cotswolds	1-85937-099-3	£14.99
Around Derby	1-85937-046-2	£12.99
Devon	1-85937-052-7	£14.99
Dorset	1-85937-075-6	£14.99
Dorset Coast	1-85937-062-4	£14.99
Around Dublin	1-85937-058-6	£12.99
East Anglia	1-85937-059-4	£14.99
Around Eastbourne	1-85937-061-6	£12.99
English Castles	1-85937-078-0	£14.99
Around Falmouth	1-85937-066-7	£12.99
Hampshire	1-85937-064-0	£14.99
Isle of Man	1-85937-065-9	£14.99
Around Maidstone	1-85937-056-X	£12.99
North Yorkshire	1-85937-048-9	£14.99
Around Nottingham	1-85937-060-8	£12.99
Around Penzance	1-85937-069-1	£12.99
Around Reading	1-85937-087-X	£12.99
Around St Ives	1-85937-068-3	£12.99
Around Salisbury	1-85937-091-8	£12.99
Around Scarborough	1-85937-104-3	£12.99
Scottish Castles	1-85937-077-2	£14.99
Around Sevenoaks and Tonbridge	1-85937-057-8	£12.99

Sheffield and S Yorkshire	1-85937-070-5	£14.99
Shropshire	1-85937-083-7	£14.99
Staffordshire	1-85937-047-0 (96pp)	£12.99
Suffolk	1-85937-074-8	£14.99
Surrey	1-85937-081-0	£14.99
Around Torbay	1-85937-063-2	£12.99
Wiltshire	1-85937-053-5	£14.99
Around Bakewell	1-85937-113-2	£12.99
Around Bournemouth	1-85937-067-5	£12.99
Cambridgeshire	1-85937-086-1	£14.99
Essex	1-85937-082-9	£14.99
Around Great Yarmouth	1-85937-085-3	£12.99
Hertfordshire	1-85937-079-9	£14.99
Isle of Wight	1-85937-114-0	£14.99
Around Lincoln	1-85937-111-6	£12.99
Oxfordshire	1-85937-076-4	£14.99
Around Shrewsbury	1-85937-110-8	£12.99
South Devon Coast	1-85937-107-8	£14.99
Around Stratford upon Avon	1-85937-098-5	£12.99
West Midlands	1-85937-109-4	£14.99

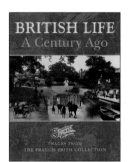

British Life A Century Ago
246 x 189mm
144pp, hardback.
Black and white
Lavishly illustrated with photos from the turn of the century, and with extensive commentary. It offers a unique insight into the social history and heritage of bygone Britain.

1-85937-103-5 £17.99

Available from your local bookshop or from the publisher

Around Bath	1-85937-097-7	£12.99	Mar
Cumbria	1-85937-101-9	£14.99	Mar
Down the Thames	1-85937-121-3	£14.99	Mar
Around Exeter	1-85937-126-4	£12.99	Mar
Greater Manchester	1-85937-108-6	£14.99	Mar
Around Harrogate	1-85937-112-4	£12.99	Mar
Around Leicester	1-85937-073-x	£12.99	Mar
Around Liverpool	1-85937-051-9	£12.99	Mar
Northumberland and Tyne & Wear			
	1-85937-072-1	£14.99	Mar
Around Oxford	1-85937-096-9	£12.99	Mar
Around Plymouth	1-85937-119-1	£12.99	Mar
Around Southport	1-85937-106-x	£12.99	Mar
Welsh Castles	1-85937-120-5	£14.99	Mar
Canals and Waterways	1-85937-129-9	£17.99	Apr
Around Guildford	1-85937-117-5	£12.99	Apr
Around Horsham	1-85937-127-2	£12.99	Apr
Around Ipswich	1-85937-133-7	£12.99	Apr
Ireland (pb)	1-85937-181-7	£9.99	Apr
London (pb)	1-85937-183-3	£9.99	Apr
New Forest	1-85937-128-0	£14.99	Apr
Around Newark	1-85937-105-1	£12.99	Apr
Around Newquay	1-85937-140-x	£12.99	Apr
Scotland (pb)	1-85937-182-5	£9.99	Apr
Around Southampton	1-85937-088-8	£12.99	Apr
Sussex (pb)	1-85937-184-1	£9.99	Apr
Around Winchester	1-85937-139-6	£12.99	Apr
Around Belfast	1-85937-094-2	£12.99	May
Colchester (pb)	1-85937-188-4	£8.99	May
Exmoor	1-85937-132-9	£14.99	May
Leicestershire (pb)	1-85937-185-x	£9.99	May
Lincolnshire	1-85937-135-3	£14.99	May
North Devon Coast	1-85937-146-9	£14.99	May
Nottinghamshire (pb)	1-85937-187-6	£9.99	May
Peak District	1-85937-100-0	£14.99	May
Around Truro	1-85937-147-7	£12.99	May
Yorkshire (pb)	1-85937-186-8	£9.99	May

Berkshire (pb)	1-85937-191-4	£9.99	Jun
Brighton (pb)	1-85937-192-2	£8.99	Jun
County Durham	1-85937-123-x	£14.99	Jun
Dartmoor	1-85937-145-0	£14.99	Jun
Down the Severn	1-85937-118-3	£14.99	Jun
East London	1-85937-080-2	£14.99	Jun
East Sussex	1-85937-130-2	£14.99	Jun
Glasgow (pb)	1-85937-190-6	£8.99	Jun
Kent (pb)	1-85937-189-2	£9.99	Jun
Kent Living Memories	1-85937-125-6	£14.99	Jun
Redhill to Reigate	1-85937-137-x	£12.99	Jun
Stone Circles & Ancient Monuments			
	1-85937-143-4	£17.99	Jun
Victorian & Edwardian Kent			
	1-85937-149-3	£14.99	Jun
Victorian & Edwardian Maritime Album			
	1-85937-144-2	£17.99	Jun
Victorian & Edwardian Yorkshire			
	1-85937-154-x	£14.99	Jun
West Sussex	1-85937-148-5	£14.99	Jun
Churches of Berkshire	1-85937-170-1	£17.99	Jul
Churches of Dorset	1-85937-172-8	£17.99	Jul
Derbyshire (pb)	1-85937-196-5	£9.99	Jul
Edinburgh (pb)	1-85937-193-0	£8.99	Jul
Folkstone	1-85937-124-8	£12.99	Jul
Gloucestershire	1-85937-102-7	£14.99	Jul
Herefordshire	1-85937-174-4	£14.99	Jul
North London	1-85937-206-6	£14.99	Jul
Norwich (pb)	1-85937-194-9	£8.99	Jul
Ports and Harbours	1-85937-208-2	£17.99	Jul
Somerset and Avon	1-85937-153-1	£14.99	Jul
South Devon Living Memories			
	1-85937-168-x	£14.99	Jul
Warwickshire (pb)	1-85937-203-1	£9.99	Jul
Worcestershire	1-85937-152-3	£14.99	Jul
Yorkshire Living Memories			
	1-85937-166-3	£14.99	Jul

FRITH PRODUCTS & SERVICES

Francis Frith would doubtless be pleased to know that the pioneering publishing venture he started in 1860 still continues today. More than a hundred and thirty years later, The Francis Frith Collection continues in the same innovative tradition and is now one of the foremost publishers of vintage photographs in the world. Some of the current activities include:

Interior Decoration

Today Frith's photographs can be seen framed and as giant wall murals in thousands of pubs, restaurants, hotels, banks, retail stores and other public buildings throughout the country. In every case they enhance the unique local atmosphere of the places they depict and provide reminders of gentler days in an increasingly busy and frenetic world.

Product Promotions

Frith products have been used by many major companies to promote the sales of their own products or to reinforce their own history and heritage. Brands include Hovis bread, Courage beers, Scots Porage Oats, Colman's mustard, Cadbury's foods, Mellow Birds coffee, Dunhill pipe tobacco, Guinness, and Bulmer's Cider.

Genealogy and Family History

As the interest in family history and roots grows world-wide, more and more people are turning to Frith's photographs of Great Britain for images of the towns, villages and streets where their ancestors lived; and, of course, photographs of the churches and chapels where their ancestors were christened, married and buried are an essential part of every genealogy tree and family album.

A series of easy-to-use CD Roms is planned for publication, and an increasing number of Frith photographs will be able to be viewed on specialist genealogy sites. A growing range of Frith books will be available on CD.

The Internet

Already thousands of Frith photographs can be viewed and purchased on the internet. By the end of the year 2000 some 60,000 Frith photographs will be available on the internet. The number of sites is constantly expanding, each focussing on different products and services from the Collection.

Some of the sites are listed below.

www.townpages.co.uk
www.icollector.com
www.barclaysquare.co.uk
www.cornwall-online.co.uk

For background information on the Collection look at the three following sites:

www.francisfrith.com
www.francisfrith.co.uk
www.frithbook.co.uk

Frith Products

All Frith photographs are available Framed or just as Mounted Prints, and can be ordered from the address below. From time to time other products - Address Books, Calendars, Table Mats, etc - are available.

For further information:
if you would like further information on any of the above aspects of the Frith business please contact us at the address below:
The Francis Frith Collection,
Frith's Barn, Teffont, Salisbury, Wiltshire,
England SP3 5QP.
Tel: +44 (0)1722 716 376 Fax: +44 (0)1722 716 881   Email: uksales@francisfrith.com

To receive your FREE Mounted Print

Mounted Print
Overall size 14 x 11 inches

Cut out this Voucher and return it with your remittance for £1.50 to cover postage and handling. Choose any photograph included in this book. Your SEPIA print will be A4 in size, and mounted in a cream mount with burgundy rule lines, overall size 14 x 11 inches.

Order additional Mounted Prints at HALF PRICE (only £7.49 each*)

If there are further pictures you would like to order, possibly as gifts for friends and family, acquire them at half price (no additional postage and handling required).

Have your Mounted Prints framed*

For an additional £14.95 per print you can have your chosen Mounted Print framed in an elegant polished wood and gilt moulding, overall size 16 x 13 inches (no additional postage and handling required).

---

* IMPORTANT!
These special prices are only available if ordered using the original voucher on this page (no copies permitted) and at the same time as your free Mounted Print, for delivery to the same address

---

Frith Collectors Guild

From time to time we publish a magazine of news and stories about Frith photographs and further special offers of Frith products. If you would like 12 months FREE membership, please return this form.

Send completed forms to:
The Francis Frith Collection, Frith s Barn, Teffont, Salisbury, Wiltshire SP3 5QP

Voucher for FREE and Reduced Price Frith Prints

Picture no.	Page number	Qty	Mounted @ £7.49	Framed + £14.95	Total Cost
		1	**Free of charge***	£	£
			£7.49	£	£
			£7.49	£	£
			£7.49	£	£
			£7.49	£	£
			£7.49	£	£
			* Post & handling		£1.50

Book Title . . . .   **Total Order Cost** | £

Please do not photocopy this voucher. Only the original is valid, so please cut it out and return it to us.

I enclose a cheque / postal order for £ . . . .
made payable to The Francis Frith Collection
OR please debit my Mastercard / Visa / Switch / Amex card

Number . . . .

Expires . . . . Signature . . . .

Name Mr/Mrs/Ms . . . .

Address . . . .

. . . .

. . . .

. . . . Postcode . . . .

Daytime Tel No . . . .   Valid to 31/12/01

The Francis Frith Collectors Guild

Please enrol me as a member for 12 months free of charge.

Name Mr/Mrs/Ms . . . .

Address . . . .

. . . .

. . . .

. . . . Postcode . . . .

Free Print - see overleaf